THE COOKIE DOUGH
LOVER'S COOKBOOK

♥

THE COOKIE DOUGH
LOVER'S COOKBOOK

recipes and photography by

LINDSAY LANDIS

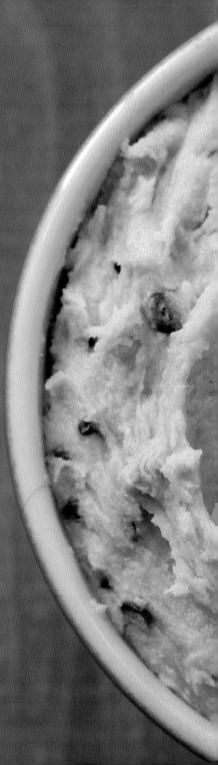

DEDICATION:

This book is dedicated to anyone who's ever been caught with a finger in the mixing bowl.

Library of Congress Cataloging in Publication Number: 2011933428

ISBN: 978-1-59474-564-5

Printed in China

Typeset in Dolce Caffe, Futura, and AW Conqueror Inline

Designed by Sugar
Production management by John J. McGurk

Quirk Books
215 Church Street
Philadelphia, PA 19106
quirkbooks.com
10 9 8 7 6 5 4 3 2 1

FROZEN TREATS

INDULGENT BREAKFASTS

FUN SNACKS AND PARTY FARE

INTRODUCTION

I LOVE COOKIE DOUGH. It's that forbidden fruit you were never supposed to eat, but you still managed to sneak a fingerful from the mixing bowl anyway. Growing up, I had my fair share of fingerfuls. My mom was the queen of chocolate chip cookies, and, as her oldest daughter, I was always by her side in the kitchen while she baked batch after batch. One time, I got caught with my whole head in the mixing bowl. Now that's true love!

When you break out those baking sheets, you may think you're craving chocolate chip cookies, but what you really want is the dough. Be honest: by the time that first batch goes into the oven, you've stuffed yourself so full of cookie dough that the final product seems like an afterthought.

After finally arriving at this realization, I decided I should save myself some time and create a recipe for raw cookie dough. Intended to be eaten as such. Unbaked. Unadulterated. Pure. The result was an egg-free dough that tastes just like Mom made it. (And since the recipe contains no eggs, there's no fear of poisoning your family or yourself with salmonella!) The next logical step was to roll the dough into balls and drench them in chocolate, and thus the Cookie Dough Truffle was born.

The success of that first recipe prompted me to take it even further—not just one indulgent cookie dough recipe, but a whole cookbook full of them. Over the past few months I've tested and retested and tested some more. I've probably eaten my weight in cookie dough, but you know what? Even after all that, I'm not sick of it. I don't think I'll ever tire of cookie dough and its many virtues: the rich buttery decadence, the gritty crunch of brown sugar, the exotic aroma of vanilla, and the joy of each and every burst of semisweet chocolate. That, my friends, is perfection.

I'm always sharing recipes and photos on my blog, Love and Olive Oil (loveandoliveoil.com). The blog started simply as an outlet to share and save recipes, to document the meals my husband and I have made. It's a personal cookbook of sorts. We're always cooking—as often as six times a week—so there's never a shortage of content. I contribute all the writing and photography, but my husband is as big a part of the blog as I am; without him, there would be no food. And the kitchen would be a wreck.

What started as a personal project has grown beyond my wildest expectations. It turns out our culinary capers are interesting to people other than my mom (though she remains one of my most loyal readers). I'm always struck by which recipes resonate most with readers—more often than not the dishes are my own favorites. Most have a pretty short shelf life: they get a few endearing comments, are reposted by a few other bloggers, and then fade into the archives. Others live in infamy. Such is the case with my Cookie Dough Truffles (page 19). That single recipe is what inspired this entire book.

So grab a spoon and join the cookie dough lover's club. (Though perhaps it should be called Cookie Dough Lovers Anonymous, but that's beside the point.) Fuel your addiction even more by visiting the companion website, CookieDoughLovers.com, where you can find goodies relating to this book and more. Keep in touch!

ACKNOWLEDGMENTS

I COULD NOT HAVE WRITTEN THIS cookbook alone. Thank you to my lovely editor, Margaret McGuire, who believed in my idea from the very beginning. She may be just as cookie dough crazed as I am. Thank you also to the rest of the Quirk Books team for producing such a beautiful book. Thank you to Jaden Hair for pointing me in the right direction. Without her I would have been stuck with an idea and nowhere to go with it. Thank you to my fabulous family, friends, fans, and new friends who helped test these recipes so thoroughly: Tabitha Tune, Leah Short, Erin Wilburn, Beth Sachan, Jaclyn Fishman, Kelly Randall, Lesley Lassiter, Liz Jenkins, Katie Bond, Holly Chewning, Crystal Jo Bruns, Mackenzie Harris, Stephanie Powell, Adrien Good, Sally Landis, and the best little sister a girl could ask for, Robin Landis. Thank you for sacrificing your time and taste buds in the name of cookie dough.

Thank you, Mom, for your encouragement, advice, and inspiration and for raising me in a world where raisins do not belong in chocolate chip cookies. But most of all, thank you for single-handedly testing a good two-thirds of the recipes in this book—and thank you, Dad, for single-handedly eating them! And finally, thank you to my husband, Taylor, for his never-ending love and support—and superhuman dishwashing skills. You know someone really loves you when they wash the same mixing bowl 132 times without complaining. Much.

I LOVE COOKIE DOUGH.

FORBIDDEN
FRUIT

YOU WEREN'T
SUPPOSED
TO EAT.

EGGLESS CHOCOLATE CHIP COOKIE DOUGH

MAKES: 1½ cups   **TOTAL TIME:** 15 minutes

- ½ cup (1 stick) unsalted butter, room temperature
- ¼ cup granulated sugar
- ½ cup light brown sugar, packed
- 2 tablespoons milk or cream
- ½ teaspoon vanilla extract
- 1¼ cups all-purpose flour
- ¼ teaspoon salt
- ½ cup mini semisweet chocolate chips

In a large bowl, beat butter and sugars with an electric mixer on medium speed until light and fluffy, 2 to 3 minutes. Mix in milk and vanilla. Stir in flour and salt and mix on low speed (or by hand) until incorporated. Stir in chocolate chips.

Dough can be enjoyed immediately or stored, covered or in an airtight container, in the refrigerator for up to 3 days.

If you love cookie dough, this recipe is the place to start! Eat it straight, use it to invent your own desserts, or mix and match the following flavors with other recipes in this book.

MORE COOKIE DOUGH FLAVORS

Vegan/Dairy-Free: Substitute dairy-free margarine (such as Earth Balance) for butter, and use your favorite milk product (soy, almond, or rice milk, for example) instead of milk or cream.

Gluten-Free: Substitute your favorite gluten-free flour mix in place of all-purpose flour. Also, be sure to choose your other ingredients wisely (e.g., chocolate chips), since not all brands are gluten-free.

Peanut Butter: Replace ¼ cup of the butter with creamy peanut butter and omit chocolate chips (unless you want them, which would also be pretty darn delicious).

White Chocolate–Macadamia Nut: Substitute mini or regular white chocolate chips for semisweet chips, and add ½ cup coarsely chopped macadamia nuts.

Inside-Out: Add ¼ cup sifted cocoa powder and reduce flour to 1 cup. Add white chocolate chips instead of semisweet.

Oatmeal Raisin: Reduce flour to ¾ cup, and add ¾ cup old-fashioned rolled oats. Substitute raisins for chocolate chips.

Sugar: Increase granulated sugar to 1 cup and omit brown sugar and chocolate chips. Increase vanilla extract to 1 teaspoon and reduce cream to 1 tablespoon.

Almond: Add ½ teaspoon almond extract and ¼ cup chopped almonds.

Gingerbread: Replace ¼ cup of the butter with molasses, and omit granulated sugar and cream. Add ½ teaspoon allspice, ½ teaspoon cinnamon, and 1 teaspoon ground ginger along with flour and salt.

Mexican Chocolate: Add ½ teaspoon ground cinnamon, ⅛ teaspoon ground cayenne (or more or less to taste), and ¼ cup sifted cocoa powder. Reduce flour to 1 cup.

SO WHAT HAPPENS IF I BAKE IT?

WELL, THE RESULT MIGHT NOT BE WHAT YOU EXPECT. The dough recipes in this book are intended to be eaten raw. Since they contain no egg, they won't bake like a typical cookie. Granted, if you add ¼ teaspoon baking soda to the basic dough, it *will* bake and you *will* end up with something that looks like a chocolate chip cookie. But it probably won't taste like what you're used to (though these do make adorable adornments; see the serving suggestion on page 64). Egg really is necessary to produce that soft and chewy chocolate chip cookie that we all know and love. If you want a more traditional recipe to bake, check out the Chocolate Chip Cookie Dough Sandwich Cookies on page 45. That they're also stuffed with raw cookie dough is a bonus.

KEY INGREDIENTS

BUTTER: All the recipes in this book are made using unsalted butter. If you have only salted, reduce the salt called for by ¼ teaspoon per stick of butter.

CANDY COATING: Instead of dealing with tempering (which can be tricky), I've elected to use chocolate candy coating. It forms a perfectly snappy shell on dipped confections like truffles. Just melt and dip (see Dipping Tips, page 20). Granted, the taste doesn't quite compare to pure chocolate, but I find it's perfectly delicious. I use the CK Products/Merckens brand, available in white, light, and dark chocolate as well as many beautiful colors. Find it at your local baking supply shop or online.

COCOA POWDER: There are two main types of cocoa powder: natural and Dutch processed. Natural cocoa powders are lighter and redder. The cocoa powder typically found in U.S. grocery stores is natural, whereas Dutch processed is more typical in Europe. In the United States, good Dutch-processed cocoa powder is sold in gourmet and specialty food stores and priced accordingly (try Ghirardelli, Scharffen Berger, and Valrhona brands). I've found that Hershey's Special Dark cocoa powder is an affordable alternative; it works beautifully in recipes that require a rich, dark chocolate color and flavor.

CHOCOLATE CHIPS: The majority of the recipes in this book call for mini chocolate morsels. I find these provide a much better dough-to-chip ratio, especially for bite-size treats. You can find semisweet mini morsels in the baking aisle of major grocery stores. White chocolate mini morsels are harder to come by; try a specialty baking or candy-supply store. Or look in your grocery's ice-cream section: Nestle recently introduced a new product called Mini Toppers, which are perfect itty-bitty white chocolate morsels. Regular-size chips or chopped white chocolate will work just fine, too.

FLOUR: I prefer unbleached all-purpose flour for baking. Using bleached may produce slightly different results; however, the differences are negligible. A few recipes in this book (such as the Brown Sugar Cookie Dough Layer Cake, page 65) specifically call for cake flour. Though all-purpose would work fine in that recipe, your cake's crumb will not be as delicate.

SALT: All the recipes in this book have been tested with Morton's brand kosher salt. If using Diamond brand, which is less salty, increase the amount of salt called for by 25 percent (1¼ teaspoons per teaspoon). If using standard iodized table salt, which has finer granules and therefore a saltier punch, reduce the amount called for by 25 percent (¾ teaspoon per teaspoon).

EQUIPMENT

CANDY THERMOMETER: A candy or deep-fry thermometer is basically a regular thermometer that can withstand much higher temperatures. For added accuracy, I prefer those with a digital readout.

CIRCLE CUTTER: A set of multisized circle cutters is extremely useful. Ateco brand makes a perfect 11-piece round cutter set that will fulfill any purpose, from doughnuts to lollipops.

DOUBLE BOILER: When you need to melt delicate ingredients like chocolate, a double boiler is key; the indirect heat from the simmering water applies heat gently and evenly. No fancy equipment necessary to make a double boiler: just use a small saucepot and a heatproof bowl (see tips, page 20).

ELECTRIC MIXER: Electric mixers make previously tedious tasks like whipping cream oh so easy. Try to pick one (stand or handheld) that comes with standard/paddle and whisk attachments. A dough hook can also be helpful when making yeast doughs like those in the doughnuts and cinnamon roll recipes (see pages 123 and 127).

FINE-MESH SIEVE: Sieves are available in many sizes, but I find my 6-inch one works perfectly for just about everything, from sifting cocoa powder to draining homemade ricotta cheese.

HEAVY BAKING SHEETS: Is there such thing as the perfect baking sheet? Nope. Some will work better for chocolate chip cookies; others produce perfect sugar cookies. Nonstick or not, I still line them with parchment paper or a silicone mat, just to be safe.

PARCHMENT PAPER: Available in the disposables aisle of any grocery store (near the aluminum foil), this is one of the most useful tools in your kitchen. It is oven safe (unlike waxed paper) and provides a perfect nonstick surface when baking everything from cookies to cake. Sheets of parchment paper can be wiped, reused multiple times, and then disposed of for easy cleanup.

PIPING BAG: Fitted with a jumbo star tip, a piping bag is the single best way to frost a cupcake. I also use mine for controlled dispensing of batters and fillings. I love my reusable cloth bag, but disposable ones work just as well and make cleanup a breeze. You can also use a zip-top plastic bag, with about ½ inch of one corner snipped off (just don't squeeze too hard, since these bags are susceptible to bursting).

CANDY

Sweet teeth, rejoice! From fudge to truffles to lighter-than-air marshmallows, these are not your ordinary saccharine treats. Go on, dig in. Discover the cookie dough secret hidden inside. It'll be love at first bite.

CHOCOLATE CHIP COOKIE DOUGH TRUFFLES

These truffles have been declared the best thing I've ever baked, even though there is technically no baking involved. They are easy to prepare and even easier to eat; as a result, it's best to serve them in the company of others so you aren't tempted—or forced—to eat them all yourself.

MAKES: 30 to 40 truffles   ACTIVE TIME: 1 hour   TOTAL TIME: 2 hours

FOR COOKIE DOUGH:

- ½ cup (1 stick) unsalted butter, room temperature
- ¼ cup granulated sugar
- ½ cup light brown sugar, packed
- 2 tablespoons milk or cream
- ½ teaspoon vanilla extract
- 1¼ cups all-purpose flour
- ½ teaspoon salt
- ½ cup mini semisweet chocolate chips

FOR CHOCOLATE COATING:

- 8 ounces dark-chocolate candy coating

In a large bowl, beat butter and sugars with an electric mixer on medium speed until light and fluffy, 2 to 3 minutes. Mix in milk and vanilla. Stir in flour and salt and mix on low speed (or by hand) until incorporated. Stir in chocolate chips. Cover and chill dough for 30 minutes or until firm enough to handle.

Form dough into 1-inch balls and arrange them on baking sheets lined with parchment paper. Place sheets in the freezer for at least 15 minutes. Meanwhile, melt chocolate candy coating in a double boiler or microwave according to package directions, being careful not to overheat it. Using a fork or dipping tool, dip truffles one at a time in candy coating to cover (see Dipping Tips, page 20). Tap fork on the edge of the bowl to shake off excess coating, and return truffles to baking sheets to set. If you have any leftover coating, transfer it to a piping bag or squeeze bottle fitted with a small round tip and pipe decorative lines over top of truffles—or simply drizzle coating with a fork for an abstract finish.

Refrigerated in an airtight container, truffles will keep for up to 1 week, though I dare you to make them last that long.

QUICK TIP:
Coatings vary on how long they take to set, so check package instructions. You can also chill briefly to expedite this process.

DIPPING TIPS:

Candy coating is a product that requires no tempering to form a hard candy shell. Candy coatings come in a variety of flavors and are available at major grocery stores, baking supply shops, and online. (The CK Products/Merckens brand is my personal favorite.) You can substitute regular semisweet or dark chocolate; but unless you want to temper it, you'll need to refrigerate the truffles after dipping to prevent the shells from melting.

For the perfect dip, use a double boiler: Bring a small pot of water to a gentle simmer. Place the candy coating pieces in a small heatproof bowl. Remove pot from heat and set bowl over pot. The residual heat from the simmering water should be enough to melt the candy coating without overheating it. The water will also keep the coating warm long enough to dip all your truffles. You can also melt the coating in the microwave, but you may need to reheat it if it hardens while you work.

If it's too thick—some brands don't melt as nicely as others, and overheating may cause a gloppy texture—thin it by adding cocoa butter, unflavored vegetable shortening, or paramount crystals, a little bit at a time, until the desired consistency is reached.

The best tool for dipping truffles is a two-pronged dipping fork, available online and in specialty candy-supply shops. The next best alternative is a regular dinner fork. Use toothpicks to help slide the truffle off the fork after dipping.

Make your own double boiler by nesting a heatproof bowl over a small pot of simmering water. You want about an inch or so of water in the pot, so that the bowl sits over, but does not touch, the water.

INSIDE-OUT COOKIE DOUGH TRUFFLES

Just when you thought Cookie Dough Truffles couldn't get any better, we turn that notion inside out. Dark, rich chocolate cookie dough on the inside, sweet white chocolate coating on the outside. You can't go wrong with this combination.

MAKES: **30 to 40 truffles**   ACTIVE TIME: **1 hour**   TOTAL TIME: **2 hours**

FOR COOKIE DOUGH:
- 1   stick (½ cup) unsalted butter, room temperature
- ½   cup granulated sugar
- ⅓   cup light brown sugar, packed
- 2   tablespoons milk or cream
- ½   teaspoon vanilla extract
- 1   cup all-purpose flour
- ⅓   cup cocoa powder, sifted
- ¼   teaspoon salt
- ½   cup mini white chocolate chips or chopped white chocolate

FOR WHITE CHOCOLATE COATING:
- 8   ounces white-chocolate candy coating

In a large bowl, beat butter and sugars with an electric mixer until light and fluffy, 2 to 3 minutes. Mix in milk and vanilla. Stir in flour, cocoa powder, and salt and mix on low speed (or by hand) until incorporated. Stir in white chocolate. Cover and chill dough for 30 minutes or until firm enough to handle.

Form dough into 1-inch balls and arrange on baking sheets lined with parchment paper. Place sheets in freezer and chill for at least 15 minutes. Melt candy coating in a double boiler or microwave according to package directions, being careful not to overheat it. Using a fork or dipping tool, dip truffles one at a time in candy coating to cover. Tap fork on the side of the bowl to remove excess coating, and return truffles to baking sheets until set. If you have any leftover coating, transfer to a piping bag or squeeze bottle fitted with a small round tip and pipe decorative lines over top of truffles.

Refrigerated in an airtight container, truffles will keep for up to 1 week.

QUICK TIP:
Look for mini white chocolate chips in specialty candy suppy shops or online. Also try the ice cream aisle—Nestle has a product called Mini Toppers, perfect for these truffles.

CRISPY PEANUT BUTTER COOKIE DOUGH CUPS

I bet you've never seen peanut butter cups like this—with salty-sweet peanut-butter cookie dough tucked inside. Just enough sugar, just enough crunch, just enough decadence. I'd take one of these over a boring chocolate bar anyday.

MAKES: 50 to 60 candy cups   ACTIVE TIME: 1½ hour   TOTAL TIME: 2 hours

FOR COOKIE DOUGH:
- ⅓ cup unsalted butter, room temperature
- ⅓ cup creamy peanut butter
- ⅓ cup granulated sugar
- ½ cup light brown sugar, packed
- 2 tablespoons milk or cream
- ½ teaspoon vanilla extract
- 1 cup all-purpose flour
- ⅛ teaspoon salt (increase to ¼ teaspoon if using unsalted peanut butter)
- ½ cup crisp rice cereal

FOR CHOCOLATE COATING:
- 1 pound dark-chocolate candy coating

SPECIAL EQUIPMENT:
- #4 fluted candy cup mold (1⅜-inch diameter)

In a large bowl, beat together butter, peanut butter, and sugars with an electric mixer on medium speed until light and fluffy, 2 to 3 minutes. Mix in milk and vanilla. Stir in flour and salt and mix on low speed (or by hand) until incorporated. Gently stir in cereal.

Melt candy coating in a double boiler or microwave according to package directions, being careful not to overheat it. Pour ½ teaspoon melted coating into each mold and use a small spoon or pastry brush to coat the sides. Reserve about half of the coating to top the cups later. Refrigerate mold briefly to set.

Gently press 1 teaspoon cookie dough into each chocolate cup. You want to fill each cup almost completely but still leave room for the final layer of chocolate.

Top each cup with another ½ teaspoon coating and spread it to the edges to fully encase filling. Chill until set, then gently remove cups from mold. Repeat with remaining dough. Refrigerated in an airtight container, cups will keep up to 3 days.

QUICK TIP:
If you don't have or can't find a fluted cup mold, mini foil baking cups set inside a mini cupcake pan will achieve similar results. Alternatively, you can make dipped candies by following the Chocolate Chip Cookie Dough Truffle instructions (page 19).

CHOCOLATE CHIP COOKIE DOUGH FUDGE

Fudge has become a substitute curse word for one simple reason: it can be a real pain to make. The slightest miscalculation can turn rich, creamy fudge into either mushy goop or a rock-hard mass. This no-fail version is so easy you'll think you did something wrong, but once you taste it you'll know it's perfect.

MAKES: **about 64 (1-inch) pieces**   ACTIVE TIME: **20 minutes**   TOTAL TIME: **3 hours**

FOR COOKIE DOUGH:
- ⅓ cup unsalted butter, room temperature
- ¼ cup granulated sugar
- ¼ cup light brown sugar, packed
- ½ teaspoon vanilla extract
- ⅛ teaspoon salt
- 2 tablespoons half-and-half
- ½ cup all-purpose flour

FOR FUDGE:
- ⅓ cup light brown sugar, packed
- ⅓ cup unsalted butter
- Pinch salt
- ⅓ cup half-and-half
- 4 to 5 cups powdered sugar (see Quick Tip)
- 1 teaspoon vanilla extract
- ½ cup mini semisweet chocolate chips

Line an 8-by-8-inch baking pan with parchment paper or buttered aluminum foil, leaving a 1-inch overhang on two sides (see tips, page 41).

Combine butter and sugars in a large bowl or the bowl of a stand mixer. Beat on medium speed until light and fluffy, 2 to 3 minutes. Mix in vanilla, salt, and half-and-half. Add flour and mix until incorporated.

To prepare the fudge base, combine brown sugar, butter, salt, and half-and-half in a saucepan. Stir over medium-low heat until butter is melted and brown sugar is dissolved. Remove from heat. Slowly stir in powdered sugar, 1 cup at a time, until mixture is smooth and sugar is incorporated. Stir in vanilla.

Add cookie dough and stir to incorporate. At this point, the mixture should have cooled to room temperature; if not, continue stirring until it's no longer warm to the touch. Fold in chocolate chips and spread fudge into the prepared pan. Chill until set, at least 3 hours. Cut into 1-inch squares and serve. Refrigerated, fudge will keep for up to 1 week.

QUICK TIP:
The consistency of this fudge is directly tied to the amount of powdered sugar you use. Using 4 cups will give you fudge that is not as sweet or as stable. That's preferable if you'll be serving the fudge directly out of the refrigerator. If you plan to let the fudge sit out for longer than 30 minutes, use more powdered sugar (4½ to 5 cups) for a firmer fudge that isn't as sticky at room temperature.

COOKIE DOUGH SWIRL MARSHMALLOWS

Some people claim they don't like marshmallows. I bet that they haven't tried a homemade marshmallow. Exceptionally moist and fluffy, made-from-scratch 'mallows are a true delight. Swirled with cookie dough and topped with chocolate chips? Even better.

MAKES: about 2 dozen marshmallows   ACTIVE TIME: 30 minutes   TOTAL TIME: 4 hours

2 tablespoons unsalted butter
½ cup powdered sugar, sifted and divided

FOR COOKIE DOUGH:
⅓ cup unsalted butter, room temperature
2 tablespoons granulated sugar
¼ cup light brown sugar, packed
2 tablespoons milk or cream
½ teaspoon vanilla extract
   Pinch salt
⅓ cup all-purpose flour

FOR MARSHMALLOWS:
2 packets unflavored gelatin
1 cup granulated sugar
¼ cup light brown sugar, packed
½ cup corn syrup
   Pinch salt
½ teaspoon vanilla extract
½ cup mini semisweet
   chocolate chips

Butter an 8-by-8-inch baking pan. Line pan with parchment paper, leaving a 1-inch overhang on two opposite sides; generously butter parchment. Liberally dust pan with ⅓ cup of the powdered sugar, making sure to coat the sides and corners.

To prepare the dough, combine butter and sugars in a large mixing bowl. Beat with an electric mixer on medium speed until light and fluffy, 2 to 3 minutes. Add milk, vanilla, and salt; mix well. Add flour and mix until incorporated.

Place ⅓ cup cold water in the bowl of a stand mixer. Sprinkle gelatin into bowl and let soften at least 5 minutes.

Combine sugars, corn syrup, and salt in a medium saucepan. Bring to a boil over medium-high heat, stirring until sugars dissolve. When mixture begins to boil, stop stirring. Cover and boil 2 minutes. Uncover and continue to boil, without stirring, until mixture reaches 238°F, about 7 to 8 minutes more. Remove from heat.

continued

COOKIE DOUGH SWIRL MARSHMALLOWS, CONT.

Place bowl with gelatin mixture on a stand mixer fitted with the whisk attachment and turn mixer to low speed. Slowly add hot sugar mixture into gelatin, pouring down the side of the bowl to prevent splattering. Increase mixer speed to medium-high and whip until mixture is thick, shiny, and lukewarm, about 13 to 15 minutes. Beat in vanilla. Drop dollops of cookie dough into marshmallow mixture and fold until dough is swirled throughout.

Pour marshmallow into the prepared pan, smoothing the top with a lightly buttered spatula. You may use your hands if that's easier; simply wet them and press marshmallow into pan. It's sticky stuff; don't worry if you can't get it all out of the bowl. Lightly dust top with the remaining powdered sugar and sprinkle with chocolate chips. Let sit, uncovered, for 3½ to 4 hours or until set.

To serve, lift marshmallow out of pan and transfer to a cutting board. Carefully peel sides of parchment. Cut into bite-size cubes using a knife or pizza cutter that has been lightly buttered and dusted with powdered sugar to prevent sticking. Serve marshmallows immediately or store in an airtight container for up to 1 week.

CREATIVE PACKAGING IDEAS:

If you are giving your baked goods as gifts, a well-thought-out presentation serves double duty: it protects your goodies and looks cute, too.

💜 Boxes. Fudge or candy boxes are perfect for smaller treats; gift or bakery boxes are better suited for cookies and cupcakes. Line them with waxed or parchment paper and arrange your goodies inside. Try sources like NashvilleWraps.com, Paper-Source.com, or CountryKitchenSA.com. Craft stores and specialty baking-supply shops usually have a good selection.

💜 Treat Bags. Clear cellophane bags are perfect for showing off your creations. Bag fragile or ornate items individually, sturdier items together, and tie with decorative ribbon or twine. Try ClearBags.com or BagsAndBowsOnline.com. Just make sure the ones you choose are food-safe.

💜 Ribbons and Twine. A simple decorative accent can take your packaging from drab to fab. Tie your bags and boxes with grosgrain or satin ribbon or baker's twine, finishing it off with a pretty bow or personalized gift tag. Take a look at BakeItPretty.com, ShopSweetLulu.com, or RibbonsAndBowsOhMy.com.

💜 Decorative Tape. Why use boring scotch tape when you can use washi? This decorative masking tape has origins in Japan, and the variety of available colors and patterns will blow your mind (and maybe your wallet). Use it to seal boxes and bags or simply as a decoration. Try CuteTape.com or ShopSweetLulu.com.

💜 Gift Tags and Labels. Whether it's the standard To/From or something more creative, gift tags are an attractive way to display the recipient's name and explain what's inside (which, with baked goods, isn't always obvious). Use recycled paper bags, old holiday cards, or scrapbook paper cut into unique shapes and strung onto ribbon or twine. Sticker or label paper, available in white, craft, or colored versions, is perfect for printing your own personalized labels. Try OnlineLabels.com.

💜 Smart Shipping. If you are mailing your treats, place the packaged gift inside a larger corrugated shipping box and pad it well with bubble wrap or packing peanuts. Air-popped popcorn (unbuttered only!) also makes a perfect, lightweight padding for delicate treats.

SUGAR COOKIE DOUGH LOLLIPOPS

Of all the stuff that's ever been served on a stick, the lollipop is the most iconic. But there's nothing ordinary about this version: disks of creamy sugar cookie dough enrobed in a dark chocolate coating and adorned with a rainbow of colored sprinkles.

MAKES: **about 30 lollipops**   ACTIVE TIME: **45 minutes**   TOTAL TIME: **2 hours**

FOR COOKIE DOUGH:

½	cup (1 stick) unsalted butter, room temperature
1	cup granulated sugar
1	tablespoon heavy cream
1	teaspoon vanilla extract
1¼	cups all-purpose flour
¼	teaspoon salt

FOR CHOCOLATE COATING:

10	ounces chocolate candy coating
	Sprinkles, for decorating (optional)

SPECIAL EQUIPMENT:

Lollipop sticks
1½-inch circle cookie cutter

In a large mixing bowl, beat butter and sugar with an electric mixer on medium speed until light and fluffy, 2 to 3 minutes. Add heavy cream and vanilla and mix well. Add flour and salt and mix, kneading with your hands if necessary, until dough comes together into a large ball.

Roll out dough between two layers of waxed paper into a disk ⅜ inch thick. Cut into 1½-inch rounds and arrange on two parchment-lined baking sheets. Keeping the rounds flat on the baking sheet, insert a lollipop stick into each round, gently pushing about 1 inch of the stick into the dough. Freeze until firm, at least 1 hour or overnight.

Melt candy coating in a double boiler or microwave according to package directions, being careful not to overheat it.

Working in small batches of 2 or 3 pops (keep remaining lollipops in the freezer), dip each one into coating, using a small spatula to cover the entire surface. Tap off excess. Decorate with sprinkles, if desired, and then arrange on another parchment-lined baking sheet. Repeat with remaining lollipops. Refrigerated, pops will keep for up to 5 days.

QUICK TIP:
A double boiler is preferable, because even after you remove it from the heat the water will keep the coating warm while you dip all the lollipops.

GINGERBREAD COOKIE DOUGH PEPPERMINT BARK

Peppermint bark is one of those things you tolerate during the holidays. It's somewhat like a fruitcake: you give it and receive it, but do you ever really eat it? But add a sprinkling of spicy gingerbread cookie dough onto a double layer of chocolaty goodness, and the once lowly peppermint bark becomes the star of the show!

MAKES: 2 pounds **ACTIVE TIME:** 30 minutes **TOTAL TIME:** 1 hour

FOR COOKIE DOUGH:

- 1 tablespoon unsalted butter, room temperature
- 3 tablespoons light brown sugar, packed
- 3 tablespoons molasses
- 1/8 teaspoon ground allspice
- 1/8 teaspoon ground cinnamon
- 1/4 teaspoon ground ginger
- 1/8 teaspoon salt
- 3/4 cup all-purpose flour

FOR PEPPERMINT BARK:

- 12 ounces (1 1/2 cups) semisweet or dark chocolate chips
- 12 ounces (1 1/2 cups) white chocolate chips
- 1/2 cup crushed peppermint candies or candy canes

Combine butter, brown sugar, and molasses in a large mixing bowl; beat with an electric mixer on medium speed until light and fluffy, 2 to 3 minutes. Add spices and salt and mix well. Add flour, 1/4 cup at a time, and mix until the dough comes together in large crumbles. Set aside.

In a microwave-safe bowl or glass measuring cup, microwave chocolate chips at half power for 2 to 3 minutes or until chocolate is almost fully melted, stirring every 15 seconds. Remove from microwave and continue to stir until chocolate is smooth. Pour onto a baking sheet lined with parchment paper or a silicone baking mat, spreading into an even layer. Chill until just set, about 10 minutes.

Repeat with white chocolate chips. Before the white chocolate layer sets, sprinkle crushed candy and gingerbread dough crumbles on top; press to adhere. Chill until set, 10 to 15 minutes, then break or cut bark into pieces. Refrigerate until ready to eat.

QUICK TIP:
Decorative cookie tins or bakery boxes turn this treat into a sweet gift. Arrange layers of bark between sheets of parchment or waxed paper to prevent sticking. You can also fill clear or patterned cellophane bags with pieces of bark and tie on festive gift tags with decorative twine or ribbon.

COOKIES & BROWNIES

Cookie dough cookies? You betcha! Despite what you may think, cookie dough pairs beautifully with its baked cousins. Whether stuffed, layered, filled, or frosted, cookies and cookie dough come together in delicious harmony.

CHOCOLATE CHIP COOKIE DOUGH BROWNIES

Talk about divine inspiration! These heavenly brownies are out of this world. A thin layer of rich, intensely chocolate brownie is topped with sweet and salty chocolate chip cookie dough and capped off with a buttery rich chocolate glaze.

MAKES: 16 brownies, or one 8-by-8-inch pan   ACTIVE TIME: 45 minutes   TOTAL TIME: 2 hours

FOR BROWNIES:
- ½ cup all-purpose flour
- 1 tablespoon dark or Dutch-processed cocoa powder
- ½ teaspoon salt
- 3½ ounces (1 bar) dark or semisweet chocolate, chopped
- ⅓ cup unsalted butter, cut into cubes
- ⅔ cup light brown sugar, packed
- 2 large eggs, lightly beaten
- 1 teaspoon vanilla

FOR COOKIE DOUGH:
- ½ cup (1 stick) unsalted butter, room temperature
- ¼ cup granulated sugar
- ½ cup light brown sugar, packed
- 2 tablespoons milk or cream
- ½ teaspoon vanilla extract
- ¾ cup all-purpose flour
- ¼ teaspoon salt
- ½ cup mini semisweet chocolate chips

FOR CHOCOLATE GLAZE:
- 3½ ounces (1 bar) dark or semisweet chocolate, chopped
- 2 tablespoons unsalted butter, cut into cubes

Preheat oven to 350°F. Line the bottom and sides of an 8-by-8-inch pan with parchment paper, leaving a slight overhang on two sides (see tips, page 41).

To make the brownies, sift together flour, cocoa powder, and salt in a small bowl and set aside. Melt chocolate and butter in a double boiler or a bowl set over a saucepan of gently simmering water. Stir until smooth, then remove from heat. Add brown sugar and whisk until sugar is dissolved and mixture has cooled slightly. Whisk in eggs and vanilla. Using a large rubber spatula, fold flour mixture into chocolate mixture until just incorporated. Pour into prepared pan. Bake 18 to 20 minutes, or until a toothpick inserted into the middle comes out clean. Transfer pan to a wire rack to cool completely.

continued

For the cookie dough, in a large mixing bowl beat together butter and sugars with an electric mixer on medium speed until light and fluffy, 2 to 3 minutes. Mix in milk and vanilla. Add flour and salt and stir until incorporated. Stir in chocolate chips. Gently spread dough onto cooled brownies, smoothing the top into an even layer. Refrigerate while you prepare the glaze.

For the glaze, gently melt chocolate and butter together in a double boiler or a small saucepan set over low heat. Stir until smooth. Pour over cookie dough, carefully spreading into a thin, even layer. Return pan to refrigerator and chill until set, about 30 minutes.

To remove brownies from pan, grasp the edges of the parchment paper and lift out the entire block. Place on a cutting board and use a large sharp knife to cut into 2-inch squares. Refrigerated in an airtight container, brownies will keep for up to 3 days.

SILVER LINING:

Many of the recipes in this book call for lining a pan with parchment paper, which helps ensure smooth removal of the pan's contents (not to mention easy cleanup).

💜 To line a square pan, cut two strips of parchment paper to the width of your pan (in this case, 8 inches).

💜 Layer the strips perpendicular inside the pan, creasing the corners. If your parchment slips around, butter the pan and between the parchment layers to keep it stuck in place.

WHITE CHOCOLATE-MACADAMIA NUT COOKIE DOUGH BLONDIES

Do blondes really have more fun? In the case of these treats, they do. Blondies are like brownies except, well, they're blonde. Replacing the chocolate with white chocolate results in a sweet and buttery cookie dough–topped treat that's dressed to impress.

MAKES: 16 blondies, or one 8-by-8-inch pan   ACTIVE TIME: 30 minutes   TOTAL TIME: 1½ hour

FOR BLONDIES:

- 5 ounces white chocolate, chopped
- ⅓ cup unsalted butter, cut into pieces
- ¼ cup granulated sugar
- ½ cup light brown sugar, packed
- 2 eggs
- 1 teaspoon vanilla extract
- 1 cup all-purpose flour
- ¼ teaspoon baking powder
- ¼ teaspoon salt

FOR COOKIE DOUGH:

- ¼ cup unsalted butter, room temperature
- 2 tablespoons granulated sugar
- ¼ cup light brown sugar, packed
- 1 tablespoon milk or cream
- ½ teaspoon vanilla extract
- ½ cup all-purpose flour
- ⅛ teaspoon salt
- ¼ cup mini white chocolate chips
- ¼ cup macadamia nuts, coarsely chopped

FOR TOPPING:

- 2 ounces white chocolate, melted (optional)

Preheat oven to 350°F. Line the bottom and sides of an 8-by-8-inch baking pan with parchment paper, leaving a slight overhang on two sides. Butter parchment.

In a double boiler or a bowl set over (but not touching) a pot of gently simmering water, melt chocolate and butter, stirring constantly, until smooth. Remove from heat and stir in sugars. At this point, the batter should have cooled slightly to just above room temperature; it may appear to separate—that's OK.

Whisk in eggs and vanilla until smooth. Add flour, baking powder, and salt and stir until just incorporated with no dry flour remaining. Pour into prepared pan.

continued

QUICK TIP:
Good-quality white chocolate is essential to make these blondies really shine. How can you judge quality? Look at the ingredients: cocoa butter should be among the first listed. If it's not, look for another brand.

WHITE CHOCOLATE-MACADAMIA NUT COOKIE DOUGH BLONDIES, CONT.

Bake 25 to 30 minutes, or until top is lightly golden and a toothpick inserted near the center comes out clean. Transfer pan to a wire rack to cool completely.

To prepare the cookie dough, in a large mixing bowl beat together butter and sugars with an electric mixer on medium speed until light and fluffy, 2 to 3 minutes. Add cream and vanilla; mix well. Add flour and salt and mix until incorporated. Stir in white chocolate chips and macadamia nuts.

Spread an even layer of dough over the cooled blondies. Drizzle with melted white chocolate, if desired. Refrigerate at least 30 minutes or until cookie dough is firm.

To remove blondies from pan, grasp the edges of the parchment paper and lift out the entire block. Place on a cutting board and use a large sharp knife to cut into 2-inch squares. Refrigerated in an airtight container, blondies will keep for up to 3 days.

CHOCOLATE CHIP COOKIE DOUGH SANDWICH COOKIES

With all the chocolate chip cookie dough in this book, it was bound to happen. Stuffing chocolate chip cookie dough between two chocolate chip cookies, that is. And I'm not sorry about it. You won't be either, once you try these twofold treats.

MAKES: **20 to 24 sandwiches**   ACTIVE TIME: **1 hour**   TOTAL TIME: **2 hours**

FOR COOKIES:

- ¾ cup (1½ sticks) unsalted butter, room temperature
- ⅔ cup granulated sugar
- ⅔ cup light brown sugar, packed
- 2 eggs
- 2 teaspoons vanilla extract
- 2 cups all-purpose flour
- ½ teaspoon baking soda
- 1 teaspoon salt
- 1½ cups mini semisweet chocolate chips

FOR COOKIE DOUGH:

- ½ cup (1 stick) unsalted butter, room temperature
- ½ cup light brown sugar, packed
- ¼ cup all-purpose flour
- ½ cup powdered sugar
- ¼ teaspoon salt
- ¼ cup heavy cream
- 1 teaspoon vanilla extract
- ½ cup mini semisweet chocolate chips

In a large mixing bowl, beat together butter and sugars until no lumps remain, 1 to 2 minutes. Beat in eggs and vanilla, scraping the sides of the bowl to make sure all ingredients are incorporated. Add flour, baking soda, and salt and mix until smooth. Stir in chocolate chips. Cover and refrigerate at least 1 hour or overnight.

Preheat oven to 350°F. Roll chilled dough into smooth, tablespoon-size balls, about 1 inch in diameter. Flatten balls slightly into ¾-inch-thick disks. Arrange about 2 inches apart on parchment-lined baking sheets. Bake 9 to 11 minutes, or until edges are lightly golden. Let cookies cool on baking sheet about 5 minutes, then transfer to a wire rack to cool completely.

To prepare the filling, beat together butter and brown sugar in a large bowl with an electric mixer on medium speed until light and fluffy, 2 to 3 minutes. Mix in flour, powdered sugar, and

continued

CHOCOLATE CHIP COOKIE DOUGH SANDWICH COOKIES. CONT.

salt on low speed until incorporated. Slowly add heavy cream and vanilla and beat until fluffy, about 2 minutes. Stir in chocolate chips.

To assemble, sandwich 1 heaping tablespoon of filling between two cookies. Press cookies lightly until filling spreads to edges. Repeat with remaining cookies. Sandwiches can be stored, refrigerated in an airtight container, for up to 3 days. Let them sit at room temperature for 30 minutes before serving.

CHILL OUT:

Unbaked cookie dough can be frozen for up to 1 month. Shape dough into balls and arrange them on a parchment-lined baking sheet. Freeze until solid, about 1 hour. Transfer balls to a zip-top freezer bag and seal tightly, removing excess air. Label bag with recipe name, oven temperature, and cook time. Frozen dough balls can be baked right out of the freezer; just arrange them on a parchment-lined baking sheet and add 2 to 3 minutes to the baking time.

COOKIE DOUGH WHOOPIE PIES

It's about time the whoopie pie, that classic New England treat with the silly name, got a bit of a twist. These soft, cakelike chocolate cookies are filled with a fluffy marshmallow cookie dough filling that will have your knees wobbling and your heart fluttering in no time.

MAKES: **20 to 24 sandwiches**   ACTIVE TIME: **45 minutes**   TOTAL TIME: **1 hour**

FOR COOKIES:

- 2 cups all-purpose flour
- 1 teaspoon baking soda
- ½ teaspoon salt
- ½ cup dark or Dutch-processed cocoa powder
- 1 teaspoon instant espresso powder
- 1 cup granulated sugar
- ¾ cup whole milk
- ⅓ cup vegetable oil
- 1 egg, lightly beaten
- 2 teaspoons vanilla extract

FOR FILLING:

- ½ cup (1 stick) unsalted butter, room temperature
- ½ cup light brown sugar, packed
- ⅓ cup all-purpose flour
- ½ teaspoon salt
- 1 (7-ounce) jar marshmallow crème
- 1 teaspoon vanilla extract
- ⅔ cup mini semisweet chocolate chips

Preheat oven to 350°F. In a large bowl, sift together flour, baking soda, salt, cocoa powder, and espresso powder. Stir in sugar. Make a well in the center of the dry ingredients and stir in milk, oil, egg, and vanilla. Stir until flour is incorporated and no large lumps remain; mixture should have the consistency of thick cake batter.

Line a baking sheet with a silicone mat. Drop batter by the tablespoonful approximately 2 inches apart. Bake 10 to 12 minutes, or until cookies are set. Let cool on baking sheet about 5 minutes, then transfer to a wire rack to cool completely. Repeat with remaining batter.

To prepare filling, beat together butter and brown sugar in a large bowl with an electric mixer on medium speed until light and fluffy, 2 to 3 minutes. Mix in flour and salt on low speed until incorporated. Add marshmallow crème and vanilla and beat until fluffy. Stir in chocolate chips.

continued

QUICK TIP:
Parchment paper will work in place of silicone mats, although cookies may stick slightly.

♥ COOKIE DOUGH WHOOPIE PIES, CONT.

To assemble whoopie pies, sandwich 1 heaping tablespoon of filling between two cookies. Press until filling spreads evenly to the edges. Repeat with remaining cookies. Refrigerated in an airtight container, whoopie pies will keep for up to 3 days.

FLYING HIGH:

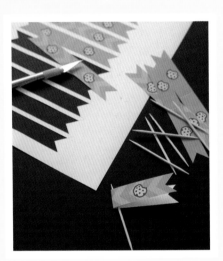

Dessert flags are a whimsical way to add festive flair to your cookie dough treats. To make the adorable ones pictured here, download the free template at CookieDoughLovers.com. Print onto sticker paper (available online or at office supply stores), cut out, and crease down the middle. Remove sticker backing (or, if you are using regular paper, apply glue to the backside), place a toothpick in the center crease, and fold, matching edges. Stick into your dessert and voilà! Instant panache!

PEANUT BUTTER AND CHOCOLATE THUMBPRINT COOKIES

With dollops of rich chocolate peanut butter cookie dough nestled atop sugar-coated peanut butter cookies, these aren't your grandma's thumbprints!

MAKES: 30 to 40 cookies   **TOTAL TIME:** 1 hour

FOR COOKIES:

- ¾ cup creamy peanut butter, room temperature
- ½ cup (1 stick) unsalted butter, room temperature
- ¾ cup granulated sugar, divided
- ½ cup light brown sugar, packed
- 1 egg
- 1 teaspoon vanilla extract
- 1¼ cup all-purpose flour
- 1 teaspoon baking soda
- ¼ teaspoon salt (increase to ½ teaspoon if using unsalted peanut butter)

FOR COOKIE DOUGH:

- 2 tablespoons creamy peanut butter, room temperature
- ½ cup (1 stick) unsalted butter
- ¼ cup granulated sugar
- ½ cup light brown sugar, packed
- ½ cup all-purpose flour
- ¼ cup cocoa powder, sifted
- ½ teaspoon salt
- 1 tablespoon cream
- 1 teaspoon vanilla extract
- ½ cup mini semisweet chocolate chips

FOR TOPPING:

- Dark or semisweet chocolate, melted (optional)

Preheat oven to 350°F. In a large mixing bowl, beat together peanut butter, butter, ½ cup of the granulated sugar, and brown sugar with an electric mixer on medium speed until light and fluffy, 1 to 2 minutes. Beat in egg and vanilla. Slowly add flour, baking soda, and salt and mix until ingredients are incorporated and dough comes together.

Roll dough by the tablespoonful into 1-inch balls. Roll balls in the remaining ¼ cup granulated sugar until evenly coated. Arrange on parchment-lined baking sheets about 2 inches apart. Lightly press down cookies using the back of a teaspoon or your thumb, slightly flattening the cookies and creating a small indentation.

continued

PEANUT BUTTER AND CHOCOLATE
THUMBPRINT COOKIES, CONT.

Bake 10 to 12 minutes, or until set. Let cool for 1 minute, then further define the indentation in the center of each cookie with the back of a teaspoon or small rounded scoop. Transfer cookies to a wire rack to cool completely.

To prepare the filling, beat together peanut butter, butter, and sugars in a large bowl with an electric mixer on medium speed until light and fluffy, 2 to 3 minutes. Mix in flour, cocoa powder, and salt on low speed. Add cream and vanilla and beat until incorporated. Stir in chocolate chips.

Drop 1 teaspoon dough onto each cooled cookie. Lightly press into indentation to adhere and then shape top of dough into a smooth dome. Drizzle with melted chocolate, if desired.

QUICK TIP:
Sticky situation? If you're having trouble getting your dough to stay stuck to your cookie, try adhering it with a small dollop of melted chocolate.

COOKIE DOUGH BILLIONAIRE BARS

For those of us blessed—or plagued, depending on how you look at it—with an entire mouth full of sweet teeth, this decadent cookie dough bar will satisfy us all. It's like a millionaire bar, but so much richer, with layer upon layer of the sweet things we crave: tender shortbread, gooey caramel, and soft cookie dough, all topped off with a dark chocolate glaze.

MAKES: 16 bars   **ACTIVE TIME:** 1 hour   **TOTAL TIME:** 3½ hours

FOR SHORTBREAD:

- ⅓ cup unsalted butter, room temperature
- ⅓ cup granulated sugar
- ½ teaspoon vanilla extract
- ¼ teaspoon salt
- 1 cup all-purpose flour

FOR CARAMEL:

- 7 ounces soft caramel candies (about 25 candies), unwrapped
- 2 tablespoons heavy cream

FOR COOKIE DOUGH:

- ½ cup (1 stick) unsalted butter, room temperature
- ¼ cup granulated sugar
- ½ cup light brown sugar, packed
- 2 tablespoons heavy cream
- ½ teaspoon vanilla extract
- ¾ cup all-purpose flour
- ⅛ teaspoon salt
- ½ cup mini semisweet chocolate chips

FOR CHOCOLATE GLAZE:

- 4 ounces semisweet or dark chocolate, chopped
- 1 tablespoon unsalted butter

Preheat oven to 350°F. Line an 8-by-8-inch square baking pan with parchment paper, leaving a 1-inch overhang on two sides (see tips, page 41).

To make the shortbread, in a mixing bowl beat together butter and sugar with an electric mixer on medium speed until light and fluffy, 2 to 3 minutes. Add vanilla and salt and beat until combined. Add flour and mix until incorporated; dough may appear slightly crumbly. Firmly press into prepared pan. Poke shallow holes into the surface of the dough with a fork or skewer. Bake 18 to 22 minutes, or until edges are lightly golden. Remove pan from oven and set on a wire rack.

continued

♥ COOKIE DOUGH BILLIONAIRE BARS, CONT.

For the caramel layer, place caramel candies in a small saucepan over medium heat. Add heavy cream and stir until completely melted. Pour hot caramel mixture over shortbread crust and spread into an even layer. Refrigerate until set, at least 1 hour. If your caramel is still soft and sticky after 1 hour, it may help to freeze it for another 15 minutes before continuing.

To prepare cookie dough, combine butter and sugars in a large mixing bowl and beat on medium speed until light and fluffy, 2 to 3 minutes. Add heavy cream and vanilla; mix well. Add flour and salt and mix on low speed until incorporated. Stir in chocolate chips. Spread cookie dough on top of caramel layer, using a spatula to smooth dough into an even layer. Refrigerate pan while you prepare the glaze.

In a small saucepan over low heat, melt chocolate and butter, stirring constantly until smooth. Spread glaze over cookie dough layer and chill until set, about 30 minutes.

To remove bars from pan, grasp the edges of the parchment paper and lift out the entire block. Place on a cutting board and use a large sharp knife to cut into 2-inch squares. Refrigerated in an airtight container, bars will keep for up to 3 days.

SOFT SUGAR COOKIES WITH COOKIE DOUGH FROSTING

What is it about the grocery-store sugar cookie—you know, the sumptuously soft, perfectly pink frosted kind—that is so incredibly addictive? Here's a recipe that's even better. Soft and puffy, sweet but not overly so, these sugar cookies are topped with fluffy cookie dough frosting and chocolate chip sprinkles.

MAKES: **about 24 cookies**   ACTIVE TIME: **1 hour**   TOTAL TIME: **1½ hours**

FOR COOKIES:

- ½ cup vegetable shortening, room temperature
- 1 cup granulated sugar
- 2 eggs
- ¼ cup heavy cream
- 1½ teaspoons vanilla extract
- ½ teaspoon salt
- ½ teaspoon baking soda
- ½ teaspoon baking powder
- 4 cups all-purpose flour (or more as needed)

FOR FROSTING:

- ¾ cup unsalted butter, room temperature
- ⅓ cup light brown sugar, packed
- ⅓ cup all-purpose flour
- ½ teaspoon salt
- 1½ teaspoons vanilla extract
- 4 cups powdered sugar, or more as needed
- ⅓ cup heavy cream
- ½ cup mini semisweet chocolate chips

In a large mixing bowl, beat together shortening and sugar on medium speed until light and fluffy, 2 to 3 minutes. Add eggs, one at a time, mixing well after each addition. Add heavy cream and vanilla and beat until smooth. Add salt, baking soda, and baking powder, followed by the flour, 1 cup at a time, mixing until dough comes together. Dough should be soft but not sticky; if it is sticky, add more flour, 1 tablespoon at a time as needed. Cover and refrigerate at least 30 minutes or overnight.

Preheat oven to 350°F.

continued

SOFT SUGAR COOKIES WITH COOKIE DOUGH FROSTING, CONT.

Roll out dough to ⅜ inch thick. Cut it into 3-inch circles and transfer to baking sheets lined with parchment paper. Bake 8 to 10 minutes, or until tops are puffed and no longer shiny and bottoms are just barely golden brown. Do not overbake. Transfer cookies to a wire rack to cool completely.

To prepare frosting, beat together butter and brown sugar in a large mixing bowl until light and fluffy, about 2 to 3 minutes. Mix in flour and salt, followed by vanilla. Add 4 cups of the powdered sugar, 1 cup at a time, mixing well after each addition. Add heavy cream and beat until fluffy. Add more powdered sugar as necessary, ¼ cup at a time, until frosting is thick yet spreadable.

With an offset spatula, spread 1 heaping tablespoon of frosting onto each cookie. Sprinkle with chocolate chips, pressing lightly so chips adhere to frosting. Refrigerated in an airtight container, frosted cookies will keep for up to 3 days.

CAKES, CUSTARDS, & PIES

Cakes, custards, and pies, oh my! These desserts are truly dressed to impress: towering layer cakes and rich custardy pies and brilliant crème brûlées. They are creamy and caramelized, decadent and distinctive, silky and sugary, and—most important—chock-full of cookie dough.